5 Secrets

Millionaires Don't

Want You to Know

Eric F Gilbert

ISBN: 978-1-968365-00-4

Dedication

For every underdog who was told they couldn't.

For every hustler who started with nothing but refused to quit.

And for anyone who ever looked around and thought, "There has to be more than this."

This book is for you.

Index

Introduction

Half the world is asking,

"How can I become a millionaire?"

Most people think you have to be born rich to be rich—or that you need some kind of special power, an elite education, rare talent, or at least the right connections in order to build real wealth.

What if I told you that's not true?

What if I told you there are five powerful secrets that almost every millionaire knows, lives by, and benefits from—but never talks about?

And what if I told you most millionaires started out exactly like you?

They didn't inherit it. They weren't born into it. But they learned these five secrets, and like keys to the kingdom, they unlocked true wealth-building for themselves.

Now you're holding those same keys in your hands.

These pages don't contain fluff, theory, or recycled motivational garbage. This is what *actually* works—what I've seen, lived, and verified. Whether you're starting from nothing or trying to level up, these five secrets will change your

life if you take them seriously.

Let's get started.

Acknowledgments

To every mentor, partner, and friend who challenged my thinking, held me accountable, and opened doors when none were visible—thank you.

To the millionaires who let me into their world, shared their real stories, and lived these secrets in silence—your examples shaped this book.

To my wife, whose faith and fire have built businesses beside me and kept me grounded when life got loud—you are

the true definition of wealth.

And to the reader holding this book:

you're not here by accident. You're here

because something inside you knows

you were meant for more. Thank you for

giving me the chance to help you unlock it.

SECRET #5:

Wealth Is Built in Silence, Not Flash

Millionaires invest or expense their money—they don't spend or consume it. While most people are thinking about how something looks, the millionaire is thinking about what it costs long-term. They avoid interest and unnecessary expenses unless there's a financial return or a legitimate business write-off. And even then, they question the value.

Usually, when you see someone dressed flashy or driving an expensive car, it doesn't mean they're wealthy—it usually means they have debt. Not all millionaires even concern themselves with their credit score. Many operate entirely in cash, or trade assets and properties instead of taking loans. While the average person worries about what others think, the millionaire focuses on the financial impact of their decisions.

Take something simple, like coffee. The average person grabs a $3 cup on their way to work so they can be seen holding it, post about it online, and talk about it during the day. A millionaire thinks about what they actually like to drink, and finds the most efficient way to prepare and carry it—without caring what anyone thinks. If that $3 is invested instead of spent daily, it adds up to over $1,000 a year. Put that $3 a day into a mutual fund averaging 10% return, and in just 10 years, it could grow to over $18,000. If they truly have a social following, they will simply post the video of them making the drink on

the machine that their corporation paid

for, because the whole thing is a tax

write for them now. That's how

millionaires think.

The Millionaire Next Door Mindset

The phrase "millionaire next door" comes from the groundbreaking book by Thomas J. Stanley, and it's not just a catchy title—it's a statistical reality. According to a comprehensive study by Ramsey Solutions that surveyed over 10,000 U.S. millionaires, 79% of them did not inherit their wealth and the majority live in modest neighborhoods. Only 23% of those surveyed reported ever having a six-figure income in a single working year.

They prioritize net worth over status signals. Instead of buying new luxury cars, they buy assets. According to the largest study of U.S. millionaires ever conducted by Ramsey Solutions, the most popular vehicle brand driven by millionaires is Toyota—practical, reliable, and not flashy. The study also found that the average millionaire drives a four-year-old car, typically costing around $20,000. Compare that to the average car payment in the U.S., which falls between $6,000 and $9,000 per year.

If we use the lower end of that range—$525 per month—and instead invest that same amount into a mutual fund averaging a 10% annual return, in just three years, that money could grow to nearly $22,000. That's enough to pay cash for your next car outright.

Even better? You can sell the old car to someone else on payments and make a profit. But if you take out a three-year loan for $525/month, you only get about $17,000 to spend—the rest goes to interest.

That's the millionaire mindset in action: avoiding consumption debt and turning everyday expenses into strategic moves that build wealth.

Why Flashy Spending is a Trap

Big purchases make you feel rich. But in reality, they often make you broke. Flash is expensive—not just in money, but in energy. Every time you make a decision to spend for status, you're training yourself to value appearance over actual wealth.

Worse yet, broadcasting your success invites the wrong kind of attention. Opportunists, fake friends, and financial predators all tend to show up when your lifestyle says "I've made it." Real wealth doesn't need to say a word.

Do you really want your friends texting

you every day asking for money? Ask

my wife how it feels. Her friends from

Jamaica see her here in the States

living a nice life, and they don't even ask

how are things, they just ask can I have

money, or clothes or minutes or a wig?

Morgan Housel put it perfectly:

"Wealth is what you don't see."

Frugality vs. Scarcity Thinking

There's a difference between being cheap and being strategic. Frugality means choosing value, longevity, and purpose over impulse. Scarcity thinking, on the other hand, is driven by fear and prevents growth.

Millionaires practice intentional spending. They might shop for sales, but they also understand the importance of investing in quality. They'll spend more for a tool that lasts 10 years, but skip the latest tech trend that becomes obsolete in one.

As **Suze Orman** said,

"Never tell anyone how much money

you make. It's nobody's business."

Don't Spend or Consume—Expense or Invest

Here's the biggest mindset gap that separates the wealthy from everyone else:

The average person spends and consumes, while the wealthy invest or expense.

To break that down: the average person works a job and pays taxes on what they make, with almost no available tax write-offs. They earn income, then pay taxes, and then try to live on what's left.

The wealthy? They have corporations and trusts for everything—and then they pay themselves to work for their own companies. It's the complete reversal of how the system treats W-2 workers.

Take me, for example. I'm sitting at my desk in my own home. All of the income I make from selling books comes directly into my marketing firm. My marketing firm then pays me a salary to sit here and write this book. That's W-2 income after the business gets all its deductions. My corporation also pays me rent to use my home office. When I drive to meetings, I log my miles as a business expense. And when we travel, I bring my camera and do a photo shoot of my wife for one of her businesses— turning the whole trip into a legitimate marketing expense.

Every dollar we spend is either an expense or an investment. That's the rule.

Oh—and here's a trick you won't hear on TikTok: every time you move money from one company to another as an expense, it reduces your overall tax liability, but all of that money stays inside your ecosystem. It never leaves your control.

As **Robert Kiyosaki** said, "It's not how much money you make, but how much

money you keep,

how hard it works for you,

and how many generations you keep it

for."

That's how the wealthy operate. Don't spend and consume—expense or invest.

And don't worry about what other people think. The opinions of broke people won't pay for your next condo on the beach.

Real Story: The Rolls-Royce Investor

The first millionaire I ever met wasn't what you'd expect. I was just 17 when I started my first cleaning business with no money, and one of my early clients had an office I cleaned weekly. His office was pristine—with things like a lambskin couch and high-end woodwork—but he wore faded blue jeans, flannel shirts, and drove an older pickup truck.

He didn't want people to know he was rich in his day-to-day life. That's how he liked it.

But here's the kicker—he had a private collection of antique Rolls Royce cars that he personally restored. Not for show, but because they went up in value every single year. While others were throwing money into flashy liabilities, he was investing in luxury that appreciated.

His quiet wealth taught me a lasting lesson: real millionaires don't flex for strangers. They move in silence and let their money speak through smart decisions.

Most people think that a car is an investment, but very few cars truly are. To understand the difference between an investment and an expense, you just need to ask one simple question – Does it go up or down in value every year? There was a time when Harley Davidson motorcycles went up in value every year. You could buy a new one, drive it for a couple of years and then go trade it in for a new one without spending any money.

If you're buying a car that goes down in value, you should never finance it! That's like paying a double penalty for the car. Instead, take what cash you have, go buy a piece of crap car to drive for the next year, but make yourself a $500 car payment into a mutual fund. At the end of the year you will have enough money to buy a nicer piece of crap that will last you 2-3 years. Keep making those payments to yourself until you can buy the $20k 4 year old car like the millionaires do.

As **Morgan Housel** wrote,

"Spending money to show people how much money you have is the fastest way to have less money."

Wealth is built through patience, discipline, and invisible daily decisions. Millionaires:

- Max out retirement accounts without posting about it
- Buy rental property while living in modest homes
- Drive vehicles they can repair themselves

- Choose utility over luxury—until luxury is irrelevant

They're not broke—they're building. And they know real freedom doesn't need to flex.

SECRET #4: The Rich Don't Work for Money They Make Money Work for Them

Robert Kiyosaki said,

"The tax code is written to benefit business owners and investors—not employees."

That single line captures the secret that most people never learn.

Napoleon Hill said it this way:

"It is literally true that you can succeed

best and quickest by helping others to

succeed."

And nothing helps people more than

creating jobs and value through

entrepreneurship.

Jeff Olson, author of *The Slight Edge*,

wrote,

"Successful people do what

unsuccessful people are not willing to

do."

And that includes taking control of how

your income is earned and taxed.

Warren Buffett summed it up best:

"If you don't find a way to make money

while you sleep, you will work until you

die."

If you haven't read **Robert Kiyosaki's**

book *Rich Dad Poor Dad*, you need to.

He does a fantastic job of breaking

down the difference between working for someone else and building wealth by letting your money make money. This is one of the biggest mindset shifts between the poor and the wealthy.

Here's the real secret: millionaires don't work jobs—not the kind you're thinking of. Yes, some millionaires have jobs, but most of the ones who built their wealth young and fast didn't get there by trading hours for dollars. That's the poor dad method. The millionaires I've known who made it in their twenties followed Robert's advice. They built systems, invested early, and let assets—not labor—produce their income.

Jobs don't just limit your income. They limit your freedom. When you work for someone else, they control the most valuable asset you have—your time. You trade five days a week, every week, for 40+ years, and hope there's something left when you're done. That's not freedom. That's a cage with benefits.

And here's where it gets worse: jobs come with tax disadvantages. People complain that the rich don't pay taxes.

That's because the tax laws were written to reward people who create wealth. When you build a business, you create jobs, you move money, and you fuel the economy. So the government incentivizes that with deductions and advantages.

But when you're working at the bottom of the ladder, you're the one paying the bill. You get taxed before you even see your money. You don't get to write off expenses, you don't get depreciation, and you certainly don't get control.

Millionaires understand this. They use time to build businesses, those businesses generate cash flow, and then they use that money to create more money—through investments, real estate, and strategic ventures. Even when they have side gigs or short-term jobs, those are temporary stepping stones, not permanent cages.

According to Ramsey Solutions' largest survey of U.S. millionaires, 93% said they got their wealth by "hard work, not big salaries or windfalls." But most of them followed the slow route—living below their means and saving for decades. That works—but that's not the path most of the millionaires I know took. They built wealth as entrepreneurs.

Personally, I never had money to save. Any money I did have, I reinvested into my companies until they were strong enough to sell. Owning your business has huge advantages, as you saw in SECRET #5. There was a time I lived on a property I owned and ran several businesses from it. One of them generated the majority of the cash flow.

So I created a property management company to manage the land. That company leased the property from me for just enough to cover all my living expenses—mortgage, utilities, food. Rental income is taxed around 3%, compared to over 20% for regular income. Then each business paid rent to that management company, which lowered their taxable profit. I structured the operations so that each business billed another one for supplies and services, shifting money legally while creating legitimate expenses.

At the end of the year, many of the businesses showed a loss, which meant I had little to no income on paper. But I still had plenty of money in the bank. As the owner, I could disperse funds when needed. And because I had no reportable income, I qualified for a range of benefits.

Don't get me wrong—I still paid plenty in taxes: property tax, payroll tax, Social Security, unemployment. But I learned something every successful entrepreneur eventually does: it's better to own your job than work one. Even better to own several—so they can

legally bill each other and keep your tax

liability low while keeping control of the

cash.

Don't feel bad if you're stuck in a job

right now. As I teach in my book *Broke*

to Business Boss, you should never

leave your job until your hustle can

replace your job. The key is to start that

hustle.

One of the millionaires I'm interviewing

for another book started out doing

landscaping, got a job as a plumber,

saved his money to buy into a company,

built that company into a powerhouse, and eventually sold it as his path to wealth. So there are many paths to becoming a millionaire—and Ramsey's research clearly proves you can get there through a job.

All I'm saying is: there are better ways.

After I sold one of my companies, I was offered a position to stay on as a manager. I took it—but quickly realized the income taxes would kill me. So I switched from being an employee to being a consultant. I billed them weekly for my time as a contractor for the same amount of money as the salary. It actually saved them money on employment taxes. Then I paid myself a lower salary from my own company, which lowered my personal tax rate. I still had access to all the money—but now, instead of being taxed as income, it was a business expense.

At the end of that year, I got the biggest tax return of my life.

SECRET #3:

Millionaires Master

Habits Before Hustles

As **Jeff Olson** wrote in *The Slight Edge*,
"Successful people do simple things that
are easy to do—but just as easy not to
do."

Before millionaires ever master
investing, scaling a business, or tax
strategy—they master themselves.
Habits are the root of success or failure.
You can't build wealth with chaotic
routines and emotional decisions.

Millionaires create systems in their personal lives just like they do in their businesses.

A big myth is that successful people are constantly grinding, fueled by motivation or passion. But the truth is, most millionaires follow a schedule and stick to it—even when they don't feel like it. It's not about working harder. It's about removing friction from your day.

Morning Rituals and Decision Fatigue

Millionaires understand that decision-making is a finite resource. The more decisions you make, the worse they get over time. That's why successful people eliminate as many small decisions as possible in the morning. Think Steve Jobs wearing the same black turtleneck every day, or Mark Zuckerberg's gray hoodie—this isn't laziness, it's efficiency.

My own morning routine is predictable on purpose: wake up, hydrate, short workout or walk, then sit down and check alerts. I don't waste energy figuring out what to eat, wear, or do first. That energy is saved for real decisions—like which stocks to buy or what chapter to write.

Time Blocking and Task Batching

Millionaires don't multitask. They batch tasks and block time. When I'm trading, I'm trading. When I'm writing, I'm writing. I don't take calls or check emails in between. One hour of focused work beats five hours of scattered activity. If you look at the calendar of any self-made millionaire, you'll find structure.

That structure builds momentum—and momentum builds wealth.

Consistency > Motivation

Motivation is nice, but it's inconsistent. Consistency, on the other hand, is the compound interest of discipline. As Darren Hardy put it in *The Compound Effect*, "Small, smart choices, completed consistently over time, will create radical differences." Wealthy people build boring routines that produce exciting results. I didn't build multiple businesses by being constantly fired up. I built them by showing up every day, even when I

didn't feel like it.

The people you see "winning" aren't

luckier than you. They're just more

consistent than you.

What Millionaires Actually Do Daily

Jeff Olson tells the story of the water hyacinth in *The Slight Edge*. This little plant doubles in size every single day. On day 20, it barely covers a square foot of pond. But by day 30, it covers the entire surface. That's how daily disciplines work. At first, it feels like you're making no progress. But if you stick with it, the results explode seemingly overnight. Millionaires know this. They don't wait for instant success—they commit to small actions that compound.

Here are some of the common habits I've learned from the millionaires I know or have interviewed:

- They schedule everything. Even rest.
- They plan their day the night before.
- They journal wins and lessons.
- They move their body daily.
- They avoid energy vampires and don't take unscheduled calls.
- They invest 30–60 minutes a day learning something new.

Jim Rohn once said,

"Formal education will make you a living; self-education will make you a fortune."

One of them even told me: "If it's not on my calendar, it doesn't exist."

That's the foundation. Master your habits—then build your hustle.

Or as **Napoleon Hill** said,

"You are the master of your destiny. You can influence, direct and control your own environment. You can make your life what you want it to be."

Real Story: From Stuck at $12M to $50M with One Change

A realtor once came to me for help with marketing. We scheduled a meeting, but he kept canceling and rescheduling. After several attempts, I finally caught up with him and asked what was going on. He told me he really needed my help because he'd been stuck at $12 million for several years and couldn't break past it. But he said he was just too busy to meet.

He even showed me his shoes— expensive dress shoes with actual holes in the soles. He said he had plenty of money to buy new ones, he just didn't have the time to go shopping. That told me everything I needed to know.

I asked if he was working all of the leads he claimed to be so busy with, and of course the answer was no. So I told him that what he needed wasn't marketing help—it was systems. Time management. Structure.

We started meeting for two hours once a week for two months. We didn't touch his marketing budget. All we did was build systems into his daily routine. The next year, he hit $20 million. The year

after that, $35 million. Then $50 million.

More importantly, he had time to take

his kids fishing and on trips to Disney.

Building wealth is about the systems

you use to manage your resources—

and your most important resource is

time.

If you don't have a list in the morning of

exactly what you're going to do today,

then you're not living a focused life.

You're reacting to randomness. And that

randomness creates stress for no

reason.

Here's a great tool to reduce anxiety: every afternoon, review your list. This is also the best time to make your list for the next day. Check if the day's tasks are realistic. Move what needs to be moved. But always finish your list. Because when you complete your daily list, you stay in control of your time. And when you control your time, you control your life.

If you don't have a list at all, then you're just chasing your tail. And you'll have no idea what you actually got done.

SECRET #2:

Information = Income

Napoleon Hill said, "An educated man is not, necessarily, one who has an abundance of general or specialized knowledge. An educated man is one who has so developed the faculties of his mind that he may acquire anything he wants."

If you want to know what someone earns, look at how they spend their free time. Millionaires don't waste hours scrolling social media or binge-watching

TV—they spend time learning. And not just casually. They invest in it.

This is one of the biggest mindset differences between average earners and high earners: millionaires are students. Not in the traditional sense— but in the practical, strategic sense.

Most millionaires I know don't have MBAs. They didn't wait for permission or get in debt to learn. They read books, take notes, attend seminars, buy courses, and pay for access to people who know more than they do. They treat information like a tool—one that can either make or cost them millions.

Why Traditional Education Falls Short

A college degree might help you get a job. But it rarely helps you build wealth. Most universities teach people how to be employees, not how to create income. That's why you'll find that many successful entrepreneurs and investors didn't finish college—or if they did, they don't credit it for their financial success.

Millionaires don't rely on outdated textbooks or theory. They learn from people who are already doing what they want to do. That means hiring coaches, joining masterminds, reading books, and taking specialized courses that solve real problems.

Turning Learning into Earning

One of the fastest ways to grow is to find someone who has already done what you're trying to do—and pay them to show you how. Whether it's through a course, a consulting call, or joining a paid group, you are buying speed. You're buying the shortcut to avoid trial and error.

I've spent tens of thousands on mentors, books, and training programs over the years. Every time I made a leap in business or trading, it was because I learned something new and applied it.

Here's the secret: money flows to clarity.

And clarity comes from education.

The more you learn, the more clearly

you see opportunities. You start seeing

trends earlier. You ask better questions.

You understand risk. You become more

confident. That's why the people who

make the most money are usually the

ones who know the most—not about

everything, but about something

specific.

Free Info Isn't Free

There's a myth out there that you can learn everything for free online. That's false. You can find *pieces* of information for free. But putting those pieces together takes time, and most of it will be wrong, outdated, or incomplete.

Millionaires don't just value education— they value **correct** education. That's why they pay. Because wasting time is more expensive than wasting money.

Warren Buffett once said, "Rich people have small TVs and big libraries. Poor people have small libraries and big

TVs." That tells you everything you need to know about priorities.

Years ago, I read about an IBM study that found 90% of their sales were being made by just 10% of their salespeople. So they studied what that top 10% did differently. What they discovered was surprising: the top closers actually worked less—but they read a book every month and kept a journal. That tells you something about the real power of consistent self-education.

Books are powerful. In fact, it was a book that changed my entire life.

As **Jeff Olson** says in *The Slight Edge*,

"People are craving a magic bullet,

when the truth is, success is always the

result of small, seemingly insignificant

steps taken consistently over time.

Books give you those steps—if you're

paying attention."

I've been an entrepreneur and a hustler

my whole life, but I never made any real

money until I started reading more—

especially when I launched my

marketing and consulting firm. One

quote in particular hit me like a freight

train: **Jim Rohn** said, "You are the

average of the five people you spend

the most time with."

That quote made me reevaluate

everyone around me. I didn't just agree

with it—I took action. I changed my

circle. That one piece of wisdom

changed everything about how I

operated, and my entire life shifted as a

result.

As far as where you get your education,

be careful. We live in an era of

information overload. You can find

content everywhere, but before you

swallow the pill, look for the proof.

Anyone can do some research and write

a book about what they *think*

millionaires do. But how many

millionaires do they actually know?

Have they ever been one themselves?

Have they built businesses or earned

their way into that circle?

Make sure you're being educated by

experience—not just by theory.

Because if you're not growing—you're

guessing. And guessing doesn't build

wealth.

SECRET #1:

Relationships

Build Riches

Your network is your net worth.

As **Napoleon Hill** said, "It is literally true that you can succeed best and quickest by helping others to succeed."

Relationships are not just part of success—they are the engine behind it. Every major leap forward in my life was the result of the right conversation with the right person at the right time.

Jim Rohn once said, "You are the average of the five people you spend the most time with." That quote changed my life—and it should change yours too.

In fact, **Earl Nightingale** said it even more plainly: "Your world is a living expression of how you are using and have used your mind."
And your mind is shaped by the voices around you.

If you're the smartest person in your circle, you're in the wrong circle.

Building wealth isn't about what you know—it's about who surrounds you, challenges you, and elevates you.

Your circle of influence is the single greatest factor in building wealth, and this is the biggest secret that nobody will ever tell—because it will change your life forever.

There's a proverb often attributed to African wisdom: **"If you want to go fast, go alone. If you want to go far, go together."** That quote captures the foundation of wealth-building through relationships. No one becomes great in isolation. You don't need to know everything—you need to know the right people. That's not just a catchy phrase—it's the truth. The fastest way to level up is to get around people who are already where you want to be. Proximity matters.

Wealthy people understand this intuitively. They don't try to do everything alone. They build partnerships, alliances, teams, and mentorship circles. You rarely find a self-made millionaire who didn't get a leg up from someone further ahead—or pull others up behind them.

Strategic Relationships vs. Social Circles

The average person hangs out with people who make them feel comfortable. Millionaires spend time with people who make them stretch.

They seek out those who challenge their thinking, share valuable insight, and open doors to new opportunities.

This doesn't mean using people. It means building **value-based relationships**. You show up with value, and you stay in rooms where value circulates. Your goal should be to give first. When you lead with value, the right people will take notice.

I've built multiple businesses just through relationships. Someone introduced me to someone else, who introduced me to a deal, which turned into a client, which turned into six

figures. That didn't happen by accident.

It happened because I stayed visible,

added value, and stayed ready.

Jim Rohn once said, "You are the

average of the five people you spend

the most time with."

I've also heard it said that your income

will be the average of your five closest

friends. That quote changed my life.

I took a hard look at my life and who my

friends were at the time. I didn't just ask

how much money they made—I asked

what kind of impact they could have on my life and business. I identified three people I already knew—but only loosely—who I felt should be in my inner circle.

I reached out to each one. I told them I wanted to get to know them better and learn from them. Over time, I built genuine relationships with each of them. One helped me become a confident public speaker and positioned me as the local Google Guru. She also introduced me to a $2M marketing firm I later purchased. Another became a mentor in both business and life. The third brought me into his world—where I met other millionaires and billionaires. We worked on multiple projects together, and he eventually made me a board member—with shares—in some of the companies we built. One of those may be going public soon.

But the greatest value wasn't money. It was mentorship. Whenever I faced a situation I didn't know how to handle, I could call him—or one of his high-powered contacts. I'd be sent to an attorney or consultant who would sit with me for hours, give me everything I

needed, and send me out the door

without a bill.

That's what they mean when they say: It's not what you know. It's who you know.

Who's In Your Circle?

Think about who you talk to about your life—good days, bad days, personal struggles, secrets. What are they doing with that information? Are they using it to build you up—or tear you down?

There was an old study—supposedly done with monkeys. Five monkeys were put in a room with a ladder and bananas on top. When one tried to climb the ladder, they all got sprayed with water.

Eventually, the monkeys stopped trying,

and anytime one tried to go for the

bananas, the others pulled him down.

Over time, one by one, all the monkeys

were replaced. But even the new

ones—who had never been sprayed—

still pulled each other down.

Another example involves fleas in a jar. Fleas can jump over 30 inches high. But if you trap them in a jar with a lid, they eventually learn not to jump past the lid. Even after the lid is removed, they continue jumping only to the previous limit. And worse, their offspring—fleas who were never in the jar—also jump to that limited height.

Your friends can be like those monkeys—or like those fleas. They may be pulling you down, limiting you, telling you not to reach, not to stretch. They'll make you late. Hold you back. Tell you a party is more important than a retreat. And as you try to climb, they'll throw your secrets back in your face to keep you grounded.

Be careful who you trust—the devil was once an angel. The saddest thing about betrayal is that it never comes from your enemies. A real friend is one who walks in when the rest of the world walks out.

Ask me how I know.

Success isn't easy—but it's worth it.

Go find new friends who will lift you up.

As **Zig Ziglar** once said, "You can have everything in life you want, if you will just help enough other people get what they want."

That's what real relationships are about—mutual growth and shared value.

And as **Les Brown** put it, "Surround yourself with people who are going to lift you higher."

Because relationships build

opportunities. Opportunities build

income. And income builds wealth.

CONCLUSION:
NOW YOU KNOW

There are two types of people who finish a book like this: those who get inspired—and those who do something with it.

Which one are you?

Because now you have the truth. No fluff. No feel-good lies. Just the five core secrets that self-made millionaires live by—whether they say them out loud or not.

Most people won't act. They'll highlight a line or two, maybe quote it on social media, then go right back to the habits that keep them broke.

But **you can't say you didn't know**.

You've seen the blueprint. You've heard the playbook. You've been warned— and equipped.

Let's be clear on what you've just learned:

SECRET #1: Relationships Build Riches

"If you're going to grow, you've got to start surrounding yourself with people who are already doing it."

— *Broke to Business Boss*

Your environment is everything. The people around you are either stretching you—or strangling your potential. Wealth starts with upgrading your circle.

SECRET #2: Information = Income

"Most people don't know how to start a business because they've never read anything about how to start a business."
— *Broke to Business Boss*

The more you learn, the more you earn. Millionaires read, study, and invest in knowledge long before they invest in stocks or real estate.

SECRET #3:

Millionaires Master Habits Before Hustles

"You're not stuck. You're just undisciplined."

— *Mind is the Matter*

Before the big checks, before the brand deals, before the business wins—there's discipline. Your habits determine your hustle's outcome.

SECRET #4:

The Rich Don't Work for Money —

They Make Money Work for Them

"The fastest way to build wealth is to own the thing that pays you instead of being the one getting paid."

— *Broke to Business Boss*

Rich people don't clock in—they cash in. They own assets, build systems, and let compound interest and automation do the work.

SECRET #5:

Wealth Is Built in Silence, Not Flash

"The people who talk the most about

money usually don't have any."

— *Broke to Business Boss*

True wealth is quiet. It doesn't need

approval or applause. It multiplies

behind the scenes—while everyone else

is fronting for followers.

What Happens Next?

This is the moment where most people stop.

They finish the book. They feel motivated. But they don't move.

Don't let that be you.

Pick one secret and live it for 30 days. Just one. Apply it. Track it. Let it challenge you. And watch what happens.

Start with your circle. Audit your habits.

Replace the noise with information. Cut

the flash. Buy back your time. Build

something that lasts.

Because no one's coming to save you.

But now—you don't need them to.

Author Bio

Eric F. Gilbert is a self-made entrepreneur, investor, and strategist who started with nothing but hustle. From cleaning houses to building million-dollar businesses, he's spent decades learning from—and working alongside—some of the most successful people in the country. As the founder of VizzyBrand and multiple other ventures, Eric has helped startups scale, corporations pivot, and everyday people escape the paycheck-to-paycheck trap. His work in business, marketing, day trading, and real estate has earned him national recognition, but what sets him apart is that he doesn't just teach success—he lives it.

When he's not building brands or mentoring entrepreneurs, Eric is fishing Florida's Gulf Coast or helping run the beauty empire he co-owns with his wife, Shana. Together, they are proof that big dreams and hard work still matter.

Sources and References

- *The Millionaire Next Door* by Thomas J. Stanley and William D. Danko

- Ramsey Solutions' National Study of Millionaires (2019)

- *Rich Dad Poor Dad* by Robert Kiyosaki

- *The Slight Edge* by Jeff Olson

- *The Compound Effect* by Darren Hardy

- *Think and Grow Rich* by Napoleon Hill

- Quotes from Warren Buffett, Jim Rohn, Zig Ziglar, Les Brown, Suze Orman, Morgan Housel, and others as cited contextually in the text

www.ingramcontent.com/pod-product-compliance
Lightning Source LLC
Chambersburg PA
CBHW031902200326
41597CB00012B/511